Animals at Home

CONTENTS

Bear Cubs	page 4
A Good Place	page 14

NATIONAL GEOGRAPHIC School Publishing
Hampton-Brown

a_e

Words with Long a

Look at each picture. Read the words.

Example:

rake

lake

gate

plane

cake

cave

High Frequency Words
because
carry
don't
new
play
sleep

Key Words

Look at the pictures. Read the sentences. Match each sentence to one of the pictures.

Cubs

1. A mother can **carry** a **new** cub.
2. The cubs **don't** sleep **because** they **play**.
3. Then they **sleep** in a cave.

Why do bears sleep in winter?

Phonics Games

NGReach.com

Bear Cubs

by Hector Montoya

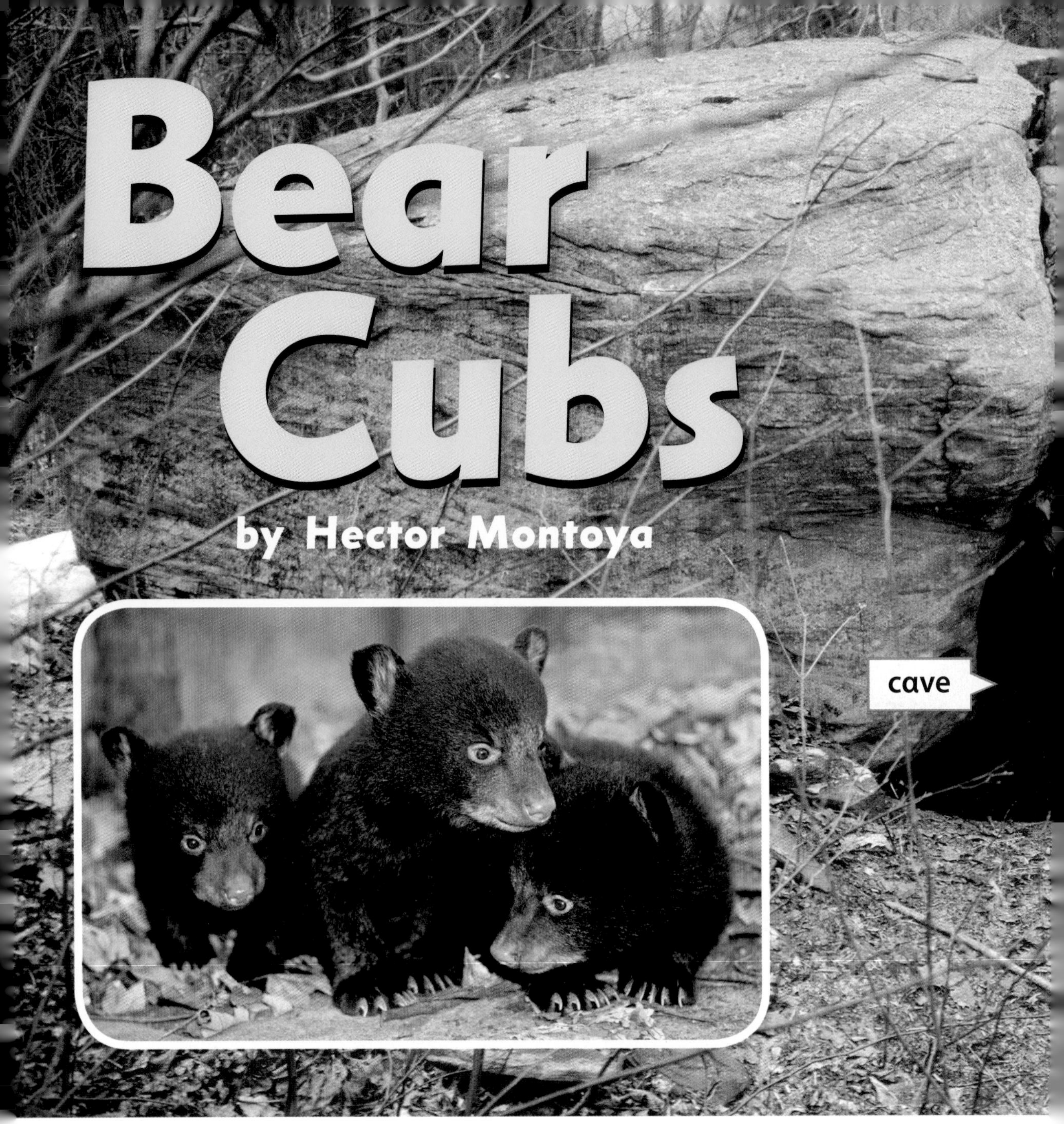

It is spring. Little bear cubs wake up. They had a long nap in the cave.

This is the mother bear. She sits in the shade. She keeps the little cubs safe.

The cubs play a game of chase.

Then the bears eat.

They wade in the lake to look for fish. The mother bear will carry the fish. Then they will all eat it. They will be fat cubs.

When winter comes, the cubs help the mother find a new cave. They find a big cave because they are big cubs.

The cubs will take a long nap next to the mother bear. They will be safe and snug together.

The cubs go to sleep. They don't wake up until spring.

Words with Long a

Read these words.

wake	lake	swim	rest
nap	game	cave	shade

Find the words with long **a**.
Use letters to build them.

c a v e

Talk Together

Choose words from the box above to tell a partner what bears do.

Bears nap in a cave.

Contractions

Look at the pictures. See how contractions are made. Read the words.

High Frequency Words
because
carry
don't
new
play
sleep

Key Words

Look at the pictures. Read the sentences. Can you find a pet to play with?

Find a Pet

1. **Don't play** with this cat **because** it isn't tame.
2. You can **carry** this **new** fish in a bag.
3. You can't **sleep** with this bear in your bed.

Which one is a pet?

Phonics Games
NGReach.com

A Good Place

by Kathryn Mead

This is a good place for my pig. It can sleep on my bed. I can carry it around.

But my bed isn't a good place for this pig! Pigs need a big pen. They like to play in the mud.

This is a good place for my new fish. It likes to play in its tank. It can swim around the rocks.

But my tank isn't a good place for this fish! Big fish can swim in the lakes. Splish! Splash!

This is a good place for a cat to sleep.
It's a soft bed.

But a house isn't a good place for this cat! It can't be in a house because it isn't tame. This big cat must run and jump. GRRRRRR!!!

What's a good place for you?

Contractions

Read these words.

it's	can't	can	hop
isn't	swim	is	big

Find the contractions.
Use letters to build them.

c a n ' t

Talk Together

This fish can't hop.

Choose words from the box above to tell a partner about fish.

Twenty Questions

Play with a partner. Choose one thing in the picture. Don't tell your partner what it is or isn't. Your partner asks questions to find out what you chose.

Can I take you to sleep with me?
Can I play a game of chase with you?
Can I carry you because you are little?
Can I wade here?
Yes, you can.
No, you can't.

Acknowledgments
Grateful acknowledgment is given to the authors, artists, photographers, museums, publishers, and agents for permission to reprint copyrighted material. Every effort has been made to secure the appropriate permission. If any omissions have been made or if corrections are required, please contact the Publisher.

Photographic Credits
CVR (Cover) Frank Pali/Shutterstock. **2** (bl) Denise Kappa/Shutterstock. (br) Ljiljana Jankovic/Shutterstock. (cl) Jorge Salcedo/iStockphoto. (cr) Ivan Cholakov/iStockphoto. (tl) Stukkey/Shutterstock. (tr) Rui Vale de Sousa/Shutterstock. **3** (b) Liz Garza Williams/Hampton-Brown/National Geographic School Publishing. (tc) Cathy & Gordon Illg. (tl) Michio/Minden Pictures/National Geographic Stock. (tr) John Pitcher/DesignPics/IPNstock. **4** (inset) Wayne Lynch/Photolibrary. **4-5** (bg) Wayne Lynch/All Canada Photos/age fotostock. **5** (inset) jim kruger/iStockphoto. **6** (b) Erwin & Peggy Bauer/Bruce Coleman/Photoshot. (t) Jeremy Koreski/Photolibrary. **7** Nancy Rotenberg/Jaynes Gallery/Danita Delimont Stock Photography. **8** Debbie Payne. **9** Eric Baccega/Nature Picture Library. **10** Michio Hoshino/Minden Pictures/National Geographic Image Collection. **11** (bc) James Hager/Robert Harding Picture Library/age fotostock. (bl) Wayne Lynch/All Canada Photos/Photolibrary. (br) Daniel J. Cox/Natural Exposures, Inc.. (t) Liz Garza Williams/Hampton-Brown/National Geographic School Publishing. **13** (b) Liz Garza Williams/Hampton-Brown/National Geographic School Publishing. (tc) Andersen Ross/Getty Images. (tl) DigitalStock/Corbis. (tr) Karin Mortimer/iStockphoto. **14** (b) Johnny Greig RFSL/Alamy Images. (t) Photolibrary. **15** Chase Swift/iStockphoto. **16** Juniors Bildarchiv/Alamy Images. **17** Wil Meinderts/Minden Pictures. **18** Juriah Mosin/Shutterstock. **19** Pradeep Kumar Saxena/iStockphoto. **20** (b) Steve Geer/iStockphoto. (c) Media Union/Shutterstock. (t) Bob Krist/National Geographic Image Collection. **21** (bc) Ken Lucas/Ardea.com. (br) Cor Bosman/iStockphoto. (br) Photodisc/Getty Images. (t) Liz Garza Williams/Hampton-Brown/National Geographic School Publishing. **23** (b) Liz Garza Williams/Hampton-Brown/National Geographic School Publishing. (t) Liz Garza Williams/Hampton-Brown/National Geographic School Publishing.

Illustrator Credits
12, 22-23 Jannie Ho

National Geographic School Publishing
Hampton-Brown
www.NGSP.com

Printed in the USA.
Quad Graphics, Leominster, MA

ISBN:978-0-7362-8034-1

18 19
12 11